914.69
JESS

PROPERTY OF SCHOOL
DISTRICT NO. 75

DATE DUE

HIGHSMITH 45-112

MANUELA lives in Portugal

Story and photographs by CAMILLA JESSEL

HASTINGS HOUSE PUBLISHERS, New York

Manuela lives in Lisbon, capital city of Portugal. Her full name is Maria Manuela. Here she is with six of her friends.

First American edition, 1969, Hastings House, Publishers, Inc., New York. Text and photographs: © 1967 by Camilla Jessel. First published by Methuen & Co., Ltd., London.
HHB edition SBN: 8038-4647-9. Library of Congress Catalog Card Number: 69-15054. *Printed in the United States of America*

Manuela's home is in the old part of the city, Alfama, built on the side of one of Lisbon's seven hills. The slopes are so steep that there are steps instead of streets.

Manuela is at the highest window, feeding her pet canaries.

As well as the canaries, she has two tame white doves.

Her father is a fisherman and is away at the nearby fishing village for most of the week. Her mother sells fish in the streets of Alfama. Manuela often helps her after school.

(The cat looks as if it wants to help with the fish, too!)

4

Because her mother is busy all day selling fish, Manuela has to do many things at home.

She does the family washing . . . and hangs it out to dry.

Often when she gets back from school, she takes care of her baby brother.

And she cleans and cuts up the fish that her own family are going to eat for supper.

Manuela's best friend is called Carlos. Sometimes she is cleaning
fish when he wants her to play ball.

"I would love to play," says Manuela, "but I must finish all my
work first."

10

Carlos has a big brother, Alvaro. The three of them often play together. Their favorite game is sliding down Alfama's steps on old planks.

Sometimes the planks are too dry and will not slide well. Then they go to a nearby faucet, take great mouthfuls of water, and spit it out carefully on to the planks.

Now they can slide very fast indeed!

Sliding makes them very hungry — just ready for the sardines that the boys' mother is cooking on charcoal by her front door.

The children put them on a chunk of bread, and pick the flesh off the bones with their fingers — delicious!

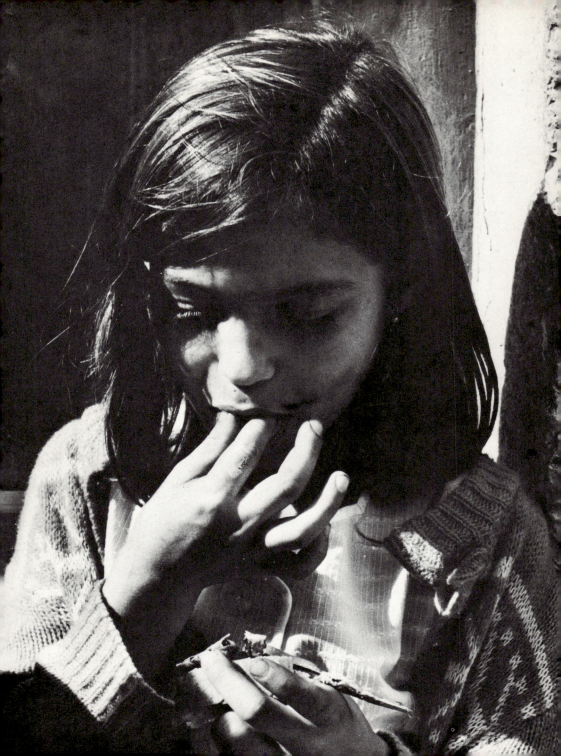

One of their favorite places is the top of their hill. Alvaro is going to climb the wall, to look at the river Tagus.

"Go on," says Manuela, "but don't fall!"

But Manuela is often busy helping her mother sell fish. She likes to go off by herself, carrying the fish on her head in a flat basket called a canastra. "Buy my pretty fish, girls," she cries in a loud voice, as she walks up and down the steps of the town.

16

Sometimes she gets tired carrying the canastra, and sits in a shady corner waiting for customers.

An old lady says her fish are too expensive.

"Oh, no," says Manuela. "They are the freshest and cheapest fish in town. And I can't sell them for less, or my mother would be angry."

18

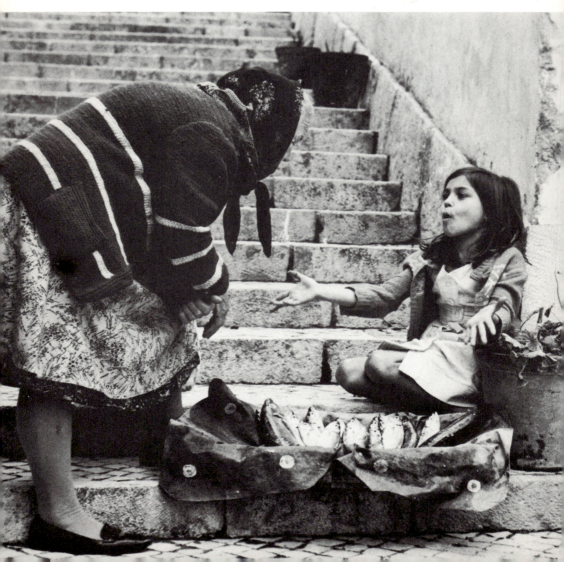

Manuela has always liked to help her mother at the fish stall too. But one afternoon she said, "The fish look so horrid and slimy like this. I wish I could go to the fishing village where Papa is, and see some live ones swimming in the sea!"

"Well," said her mother, "perhaps one day I can take you."

The next morning, Manuela was sitting and dreaming of her visit to the fishing village, when she heard a shout from Carlos.

21

Off they went together, and met Alvaro on their way. Manuela told the boys how much she wanted to go to the village where her father kept his boat.

"Can't we come too? Why can't we all go together?" they asked.

"Yes, why not? Perhaps we could go today!" said Manuela.

They ran to find Manuela's mother.

When they got to her home, Manuela shouted, "Ma, where are you?" But there was no reply.

She went to ask her grandmother, who was sitting on a nearby

door-step with Manuela's baby brother.

"Your mother has gone to the fish market to buy fish to sell," said Grannie.

"I must find her," cried Manuela. "You wait for me at home," she told the boys. She rushed off.

As she ran, she began to wonder if she was quite sure of the way to the fish market.

Then, in the far distance, under an archway, she thought she saw her mother with her canastra on her head.

She ran and ran until she caught up with her. But it was not her mother. It was a complete stranger . . .

Manuela walked and walked. She reached the modern part of the city. There were so many people and so many cars.

Suddenly Manuela was frightened. She had no idea where to find the fish market.

29

Outside the gates of a great palace, she saw soldiers on guard.
She went up and asked one of them the way. But he was on duty.
He kept his nose in the air, and pretended not to hear her.

Then she saw a flower-seller and asked her. The flower-seller said, "Dear me, little girl, you shouldn't be wandering round the town alone. You go home, and wait for your mother there."

Manuela did not know the way home any better than she knew the way to the fish market. So she plucked up courage, and went to ask the traffic policeman who was standing high on a platform under a huge umbrella. The policeman pointed out the right way.

But when she reached the fish market, her troubles were not over. There were so many people . . .

. . . and so many fish! She saw boxes and boxes of sardines, some of them to be eaten by Portuguese people like herself — and more, she knew, to be put into tins and sent all over the world.

Suddenly she saw her mother among a crowd of friends.

"Oh," she said, "I was so afraid I might not find you." Then quickly she asked, "Ma, will you take me to the fishing village today?"

"No, not today," said her mother. "Look at all these fish I've bought in the market. Now I have to sell them."

"Well, could I go with Carlos and Alvaro to the village?"

Her mother saw how much she wanted to go. "Yes, why not," she said. Manuela gave her a big hug. They got a ride home in a truck.

Manuela's mother helped her change into her best dress. "You must wear your shawl," she said. "It's autumn now." Manuela was in such a hurry to go, she hardly heard.

The boys had been waiting all this time, brushed, scrubbed and ready.

"I don't think she will ever come," said Alvaro.

But suddenly there she was, looking very pretty indeed.

They walked quickly to the station and took the train out of Lisbon, past the mouth of the river, and along by the open sea.

At last they arrived at the fishing village.

There Manuela's father and his shipmate were busy working with their small fishing boat on the beach.

Manuela's father was surprised to see her!

Manuela was fascinated to see him patching up his fishing net.

"I didn't know that men could do mending," she said. "You had better show me how, Papa."

Even though the boat was on shore, the boys wanted to try rowing.

The shipmate brought them two fishermen's caps! They felt like real sailors.

Manuela was getting impatient. Half the afternoon was gone, and still they had not even started to look for live fish in the sea.

The men were too busy getting ready for the evening's fishing to take the children out in the boat. So they pulled in a boat that was anchored near by. Alvaro held on to it while the others climbed in.

Carlos and Manuela looked over the side and saw the live fish gliding below. They trailed their hands in the water, but they could not catch any.

So they climbed out again, and hunted at the water's edge.

"Look," cried Manuela, "here's a fish."

"Hah!" said Alvaro. "It's just a dead fish floating."

But a few minutes later, a big wave came and knocked Alvaro right over into the sea. They all laughed and laughed. "Who's floating now?" Manuela cried, as he struggled to get up.

46

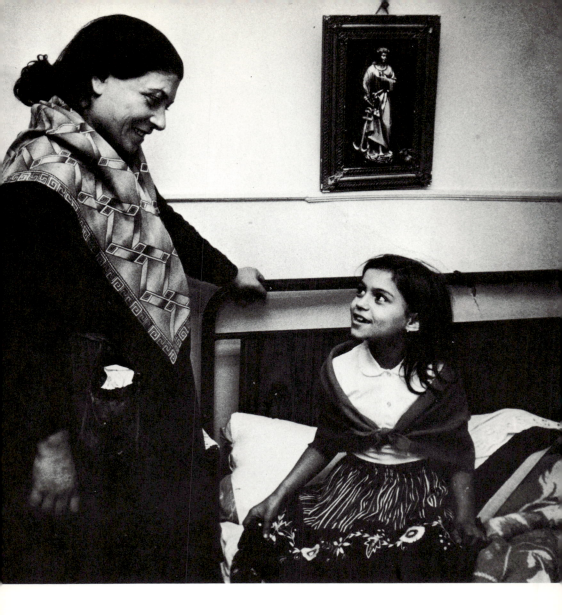

When she got home that night, Manuela's mother asked her, "Well then, did you see any live fish swimming in the sea?"

"Yes," replied Manuela, "but only little ones. The largest thing I saw floating in the sea was Alvaro!"